2760

RECEIVED JUL 1 1 2019

INDEX

A
Articles of Confederation, 6, 7, 8, 28

C
Congress, U.S., 7, 10, 12, 13, 14, 20, 22, 24, 25, 30
Constitution, U.S., 6, 7, 8, 9, 10, 11, 16, 18, 20, 22, 28, 30
Constitutional Convention, 6, 8, 9, 30

D
Declaration of Independence, 4, 5

E
Electoral College, 20
executive branch, 10, 12, 14, 16, 22, 24
executive orders, 16, 22, 23, 30
executive privilege, 22

F
federalism, 18

G
Great Britain, 4
Great Compromise, 7

H
House of Representatives, 7, 10, 13, 14, 24, 25

J
judicial branch, 10, 12, 14, 16, 24
judicial review, 16

L
legislative branch, 10, 12, 14, 16, 24

P
president, 10, 12, 14, 15, 20, 21, 22, 23, 24

R
republican government, 10, 11

S
Senate, U.S., 7, 10, 12, 13, 14, 16, 30
Supreme Court, U.S., 10, 12, 14, 16, 17, 24, 25, 30

T
10th Amendment, 20

WEBSITES

Due to the changing nature of Internet links, PowerKids Press has developed an online list of websites related to the subject of this book. This site is updated regularly. Please use this link to access the list: www.powerkidslinks.com/kqah/power

GLOSSARY

amendment: A change in the words or meaning of a law or document, such as a constitution.

behalf: In a person's interest or support.

bill: A draft of a law presented to a legislature for consideration.

compromise: An agreement in which each person or group gives up something in order to end a dispute.

convention: A meeting of people for a common purpose.

delegate: A person sent to a meeting or convention to represent others.

draft: A piece of writing written earlier than the piece of writing that is actually submitted.

impeach: To charge a public official with a crime done while in office.

internment camp: A place where people, such as Japanese Americans during World War II, are forced to live and work.

investigate: To try to find out the facts about something.

monarchy: A form of government headed by a king or queen.

segregation: The separation of people based on race, class, or ethnicity.

violation: The act of ignoring or interfering with a person's rights.

virtue: Morally good behavior or character.

TIMELINE

SEPTEMBER 17, 1787
Delegates to the Constitutional Convention sign the U.S Constitution.

MARCH 4, 1789
Congress meets for the first time.

FEBRUARY 2, 1790
The Supreme Court holds its first session.

JANUARY 1, 1863
President Lincoln's Emancipation Proclamation, an executive order, goes into effect.

1865-1869
President Andrew Johnson vetoes 21 bills. Congress overrides 15 of them.

MAY 18, 1896
The Supreme Court rules that "separate but equal" facilities are constitutional and legal in *Plessy v. Ferguson*.

MAY 17, 1954
The Supreme Court overturns *Plessy v. Ferguson*, saying that racial segregation is unconstitutional and illegal in *Brown v. Board of Education of Topeka*.

JUNE 30, 1971
The Supreme Court allows two newspapers to publish secret government information about the Vietnam War, saying they are exercising their First Amendment rights.

OCTOBER 23, 1987
The Senate rejects Robert Bork, President Reagan's nominee for Supreme Court, by the largest margin in history

MAY 7, 1992
The 27th Amendment is passed 203 years after James Madison proposed it in 1789. The amendment bans pay increases or decreases for members of Congress from taking effect until after the next election.

OCTOBER 26, 2001
President George W. Bush signs the Patriot Act. Among other things, this act allows the government to search homes or businesses without permission.

JANUARY 20, 2017-OCTOBER 13, 2017
President Trump signs 49 executive orders.

INDEPENDENCE HALL, PHILADELPHIA

EVEN THOUGH IT MAY SOMETIMES SEEM LIKE POWER ISN'T BALANCED IN THE U.S. GOVERNMENT, PEOPLE CAN USE THEIR OWN POWER TO VOTE ON THE PRESIDENT AND THEIR REPRESENTATIVES.

IS GOVERNMENT BALANCED?

Doing away with the Articles of Confederation and creating the U.S. Constitution gave the federal government more power. However, the framers of the Constitution didn't want one person or group of people to have all the power. This is why they created a system of checks and balances. But is the balance of power in government truly balanced?

Our system of checks and balances prevents one branch of government from getting too powerful by giving the other two ways to check it. This doesn't mean that the branches of government haven't found ways around the other branches' checks. Sometimes, the checking process takes a long time to happen or produce results. However, as long as citizens continue to exercise their right to check on the government through voting for what they believe in, the system of checks and balances will keep working to prevent one branch of the U.S. government from having too much power.

WHICH LAW DO I FOLLOW?

Different levels of legislative power can cause confusion between state and federal laws. For instance, federal law states that service animals, such as dogs that help guide blind people, must be allowed in all public buildings. This law also makes it illegal to ask for proof that an animal is a trained service animal. Federal law must always be followed over state law. However, 19 states have passed laws that make it illegal to misrepresent an animal as a service animal. This can be punished with a fine, community service, or criminal charges.

STATE VS. FEDERAL LAW

The growth of legislative power has been a comfort to some people and a threat to others. Some people believe a larger federal government is better equipped to help people. They also think the federal government should set strict rules for businesses such as banks and factories to protect people's safety and well-being.

Other people believe the federal government should have less control over issues that could be regulated by the states. For example, some people believe businesses should be left alone to run themselves. Some people also believe the state and local governments are better at making laws for their people because each state has different needs. Local lawmakers may understand those needs better.

PEOPLE'S IDEA OF HOW LARGE GOVERNMENT SHOULD BE OFTEN DEPENDS ON WHICH POLITICAL PARTY THEY ARE A PART OF. DEMOCRATS TEND TO WANT A STRONG FEDERAL GOVERNMENT, WHILE REPUBLICANS TEND TO WANT THE STATES TO HAVE MORE POWER.

INS V. CHADHA

Jagdish Rai Chadha came into the United States with a student visa and stayed longer than it allowed. When the U.S. Immigration and Naturalization Service (INS) moved to deport him, Chadha asked the INS to suspend his deportation. The U.S. attorney general approved the suspension and reported it to Congress. The House of Representatives vetoed the attorney general's ruling. Chadha's case was sent back to immigration court. He appealed the ruling and the case eventually reached the U.S. Supreme Court.

STUDENT VISAS MAKE IT POSSIBLE FOR PEOPLE FROM OTHER COUNTRIES TO COME TO THE UNITED STATES TO STUDY SUBJECTS THEY MIGHT NOT BE ABLE TO STUDY IN THEIR HOME COUNTRY.

STUDENT VISA

AVOIDING CHECKS

Congress also has ways to get around some of the other branches' checks. Legislative vetoes, where Congress overturns a presidential veto with a two-thirds vote in both chambers, are one example. By vetoing a bill, the president is checking the legislative branch. By vetoing the president's veto, Congress avoids being checked.

In 1983, the Supreme Court ruled in *INS v. Chadha* that a House of Representatives veto of a ruling by the U.S. attorney general, or chief law officer, was unconstitutional. The attorney general is a member of the executive branch. The House's veto was originally allowed due to the wording of the Immigration and Nationality Act, which gave Congress the power to veto executive actions with only one chamber rather than both chambers. The ruling of *INS v. Chadha* was a way for the judicial branch to check Congress.

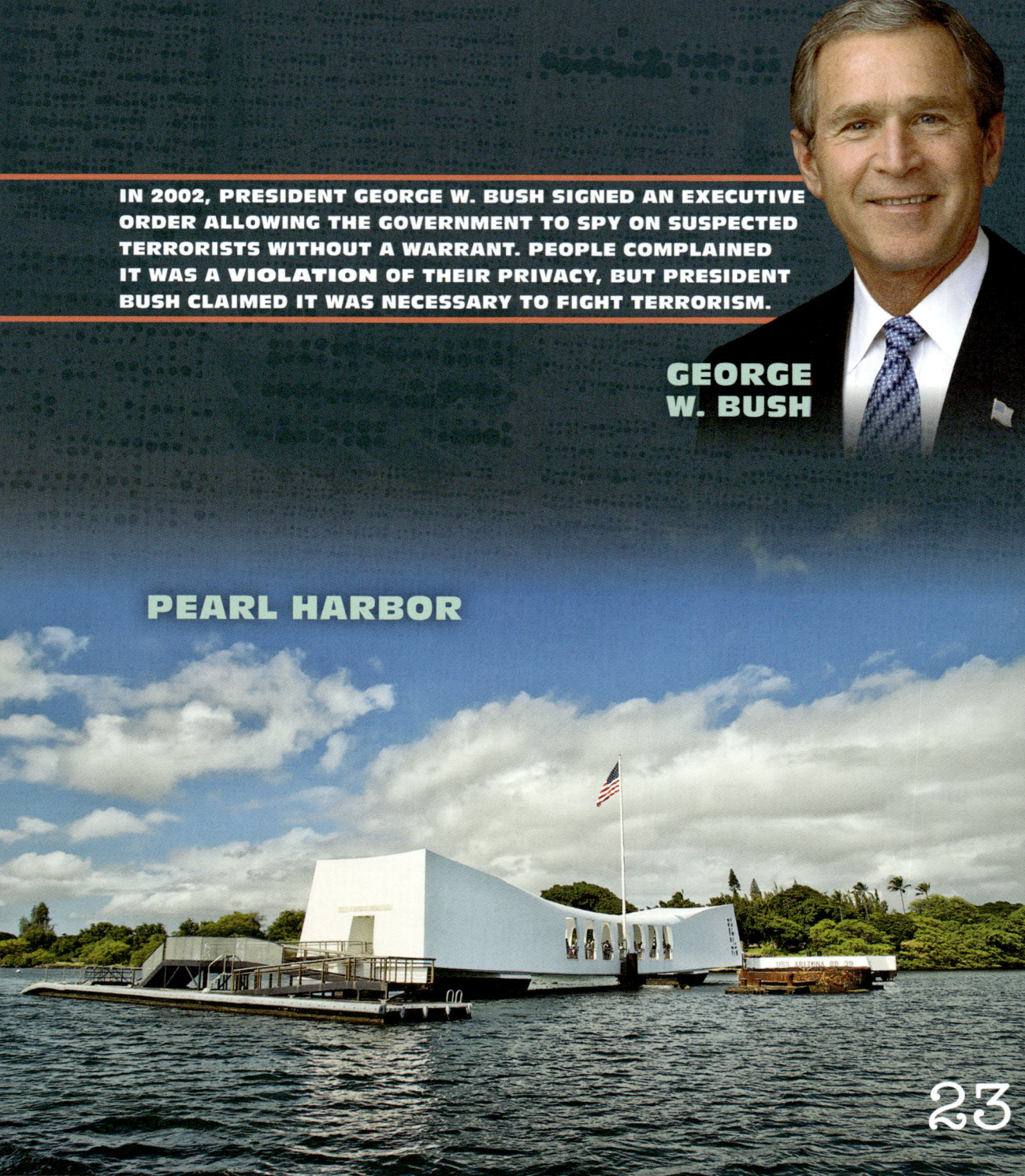

IN 2002, PRESIDENT GEORGE W. BUSH SIGNED AN EXECUTIVE ORDER ALLOWING THE GOVERNMENT TO SPY ON SUSPECTED TERRORISTS WITHOUT A WARRANT. PEOPLE COMPLAINED IT WAS A **VIOLATION** OF THEIR PRIVACY, BUT PRESIDENT BUSH CLAIMED IT WAS NECESSARY TO FIGHT TERRORISM.

GEORGE W. BUSH

PEARL HARBOR

PRESIDENTIAL POWER

The framers of the U.S. Constitution knew how dangerous power can be if only one person has it. This is why a system of checks and balances is so important. However, little by little, the executive branch has increased its power in the U.S. government.

The president can issue orders to federal agencies and employees. These are called executive orders. This means that the executive branch may issue orders that are much like laws without checks from Congress if it feels that it's in the best interest of U.S. citizens.

Executive privilege allows the president to keep information from Congress and the courts. Presidents usually claim executive privilege by saying the release of certain information would hurt national security.

HISTORIC MOMENTS

After the Japanese military attacked a U.S. naval base near Pearl Harbor, Hawaii, on December 7, 1941, President Franklin D. Roosevelt gave an executive order forcing over 120,000 Japanese Americans to be held in **internment camps** against their will.

HILLARY CLINTON

DONALD TRUMP

HISTORIC MOMENTS

It's possible to lose the popular vote and still be elected president through electoral votes. In 2016, President Donald Trump lost the popular vote to Hillary Clinton by almost 2.9 million votes. However, he won the presidential election with 306 electoral votes.

KEEPING THE PEOPLE IN CHECK

The Constitution also checks the power of citizens. The presidential election process is a check on the people. The people don't directly elect the president. A group of appointed representatives from each state elect the president. This group of electors is called the Electoral College. Each state's number of electoral votes is based on how many members of Congress the state has. Usually, whichever presidential candidate wins the most votes in a state gets all of that state's electoral votes.

Citizens have the right to check the power of the government. Citizens check the government by exercising their right to vote and electing members of government. Other checks include the right to gather as a group and the freedom to give opinions about how government runs without worrying about punishment.

THE PRESS IS LIKE THE VOICE OF THE PEOPLE, WHICH HELPS KEEP GOVERNMENT IN CHECK. REPORTERS WHO SUSPECT THE GOVERNMENT OF COVERING UP CRIMES ARE FREE TO INVESTIGATE AND INFORM PEOPLE OF WRONGDOING.

STATE GOVERNMENTS ARE RESPONSIBLE FOR GIVING PEOPLE THEIR DRIVER'S LICENSES. THEY ALSO GIVE OUT MARRIAGE AND HUNTING LICENSES.

ABRAHAM LINCOLN

HISTORIC MOMENTS

After the election of Abraham Lincoln as president in 1860, 11 Southern states seceded, or broke away, from the Union and formed the Confederate States of America. Leaders in these states felt that, because they disagreed with the federal government, they were constitutionally able to secede.

FEDERALISM

Under the Constitution, the United States has a system of federalism, which means power is divided between the federal government and the state governments. The Constitution gives specific powers to the federal government, including printing money, declaring war, and managing trade with other nations.

The 10th **Amendment** to the Constitution gives all powers not given to the federal government to the states. States must follow the Constitution but have the right to control other things within their borders, including taxes, education, transportation, and public safety.

State governments are set up much like the federal government. Each state has a constitution, legislature, and supreme court. In addition, each branch of the state government has checks and balances similar to those of the federal government.

CHANGING LAWS FOR EQUAL RIGHTS

In 1892, Homer Plessy, an African American man, refused to leave his seat in a whites-only car on a Louisiana train. The case *Plessy v. Ferguson* went to the Supreme Court. On May 18, 1896, the Supreme Court ruled that "separate but equal" facilities made racial **segregation** legal. However, on May 17, 1954, the Supreme Court ruled differently in *Brown v. Board of Education of Topeka*, a case about allowing African American students in whites-only public schools. This case overturned *Plessy v. Ferguson*, stating that "separate but equal" facilities are unconstitutional and illegal.

PLESSY V. FERGUSON
PRESS STREET RAILROAD YARDS
Site of the Arrest of Homer Adolph Plessy

On June 7, 1892, Homer Adolph Plessy was removed from the East Louisiana Railroad train and arrested by Detective C.C. Cain at the corner of Royal and Press St. He was charged with violating the 1890 Louisiana Separate Car Act that separated railroad passengers by race.

Plessy's act of civil disobedience was a test case organized by the Comité des Citoyens (Citizens' Committee) whose aim was to overturn segregation laws that were being enacted across the South. The philosophy and strategies of the Comité des Citoyens foreshadowed Civil Rights movements of the 20th century. Although the Supreme Court ruled against Plessy on May 18, 1896, his case marked the first post-Reconstruction use of the 14th Amendment's "equal protection" provision in a legal challenge to segregation. In their final statement after the Supreme Court verdict, the Comité des Citoyens proclaimed, "We as freemen still believe we were right and our cause is sacred...In defending the cause of liberty, we met with defeat but not with ignominy". Their position was vindicated when the Supreme Court upheld similar 14th Amendment arguments in the 1954 case of Brown v. Board of Education.
(Continued on other side)

CRESCENT CITY PEACE ALLIANCE

SUPREME COURT 2017

JUDICIAL BRANCH

The Supreme Court, the highest court in the United States, heads the judicial branch. The judicial branch, which is made up of federal courts, examines and explains the laws in the Constitution and rules on cases involving states. The executive branch appoints judges to the Supreme Court and the Senate approves them. Supreme Court justices hold their positions for life. However, they can resign or be impeached.

One check on both the executive and legislative branches is called judicial review. This allows the Supreme Court to overturn laws or executive orders that don't follow the Constitution. The only way a Supreme Court decision can be changed is by changing the Constitution or if the Supreme Court rules against itself in a later case.

AS OF APRIL 2017, THERE HAVE BEEN 113 SUPREME COURT JUSTICES. ON AVERAGE, SUPREME COURT JUSTICES SERVE 16 YEARS.

FRANKLIN D. ROOSEVELT VETOED MORE LAWS THAN ANY OTHER PRESIDENT WITH 635 VETOES DURING HIS FOUR TERMS.

FRANKLIN D. ROOSEVELT

PRESIDENT BARACK OBAMA'S CABINET 2009

EXECUTIVE BRANCH

The job of the executive branch, led by the president, is to carry out laws, deal with foreign nations, and lead the military. Although the legislative branch makes the laws, the executive branch has the power to veto those laws. The executive branch can also recommend laws. It can call special meetings for Congress to discuss legislation, or laws. The president also selects a cabinet, which is made up of the leaders of each department in the White House. Congress, however, must approve these people.

The executive branch checks the judicial branch by nominating judges to the Supreme Court and federal court system. The Senate must approve the president's judicial nominations. The president can also pardon some people who have committed crimes.

HISTORIC MOMENTS

Only two presidents have ever been impeached: Andrew Johnson in 1868 and Bill Clinton in 1998. The Senate found both not guilty. Richard Nixon was almost impeached in 1974, but he resigned from office before the House finished the impeachment proceedings.

CONGRESS ALSO HOLDS COMMITTEE AND SUBCOMMITTEE HEARINGS. EACH CHAMBER HAS SPECIAL COMMITTEES THAT GO OVER THE BILLS PROPOSED IN SUBCOMMITTEES. DURING HEARINGS, THE GROUP TALKS ABOUT THE GOOD AND BAD ASPECTS OF EACH BILL.

CHECKING CONGRESS

Congress has the ability to perform checks and balances on itself. The House of Representatives is the only body that can propose revenue bills, or bills about the government's income. From the House, the bill goes to the Senate. If the Senate doesn't approve the bill, it's sent back to the House for changes. Bills that start in the Senate must receive approval from the House. This keeps Congress in check so that one chamber can't hold its power over the other chamber.

LEGISLATIVE BRANCH

The legislative branch is responsible for making and changing laws, declaring war, and deciding how the nation spends its money.

The legislative branch can overturn a president's veto, or rejection, of a **bill** with a two-thirds vote from both chambers. Congress may also **investigate** the actions of the executive branch and even **impeach** the president. The Senate has the power to approve the appointments of some of the members of the president's cabinet and approve treaties the United States makes with other countries. Congress also has control of the country's money and decides how much can be put toward certain government actions.

The legislative branch's checks on the judicial branch include the ability to approve and impeach Supreme Court justices and the right to create lower courts.

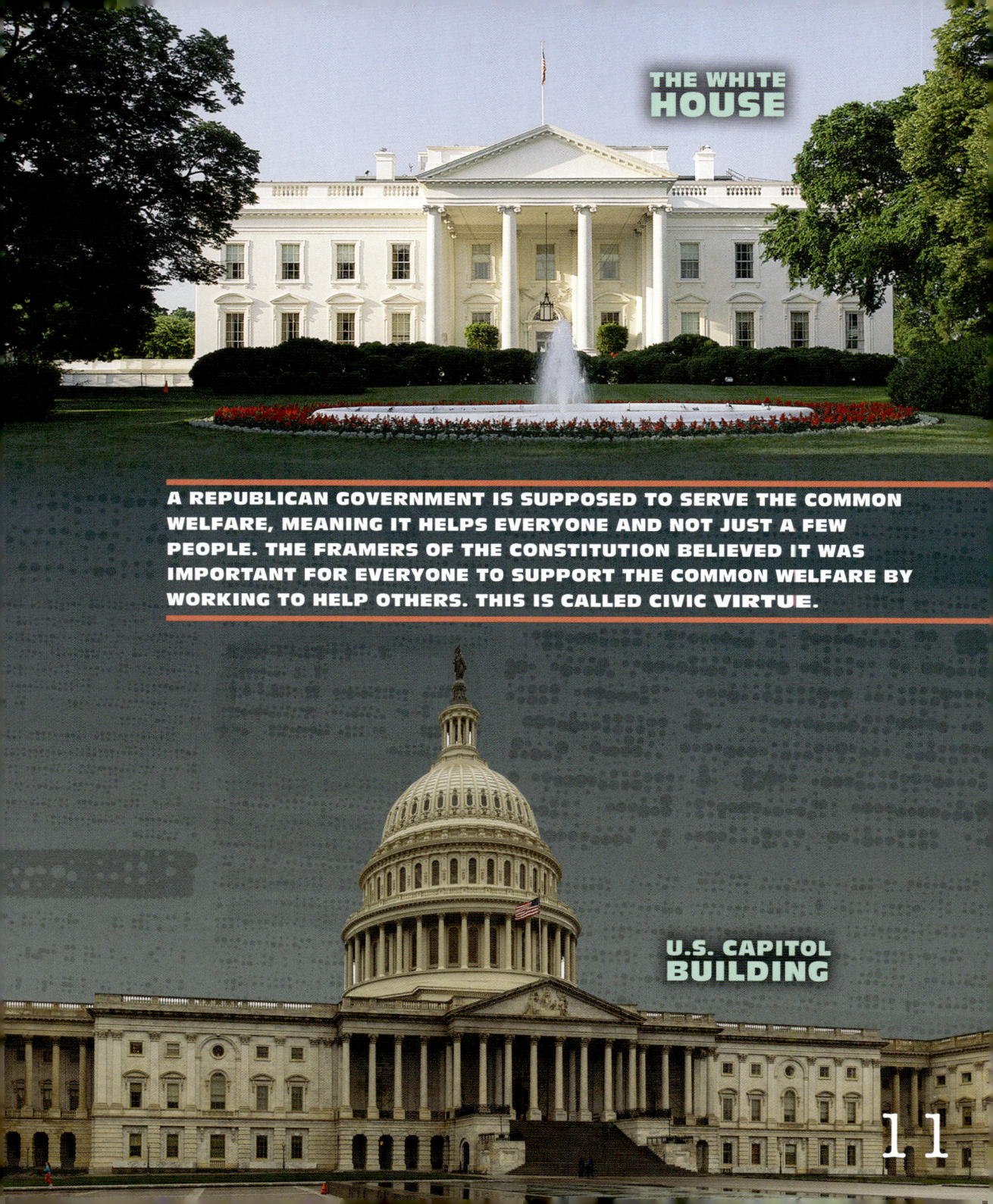

THE WHITE HOUSE

A REPUBLICAN GOVERNMENT IS SUPPOSED TO SERVE THE COMMON WELFARE, MEANING IT HELPS EVERYONE AND NOT JUST A FEW PEOPLE. THE FRAMERS OF THE CONSTITUTION BELIEVED IT WAS IMPORTANT FOR EVERYONE TO SUPPORT THE COMMON WELFARE BY WORKING TO HELP OTHERS. THIS IS CALLED CIVIC VIRTUE.

U.S. CAPITOL BUILDING

SEPARATION OF POWER

The framers of the U.S. Constitution created a system of separation of powers enforced through checks and balances as part of a republican government. A republican government gives people the power to elect leaders to make choices on the citizens' **behalf**. These leaders should create and pass laws that are in the best interest of all citizens.

Each branch of the government consists of different people with different jobs. The executive branch consists of the president and his or her cabinet. The legislative branch consists of the Senate and the House of Representatives, which are called Congress. The judicial branch is made up of the Supreme Court justices and other federal courts. Each group has powers to make sure the others follow the rules.

SUPREME COURT BUILDING

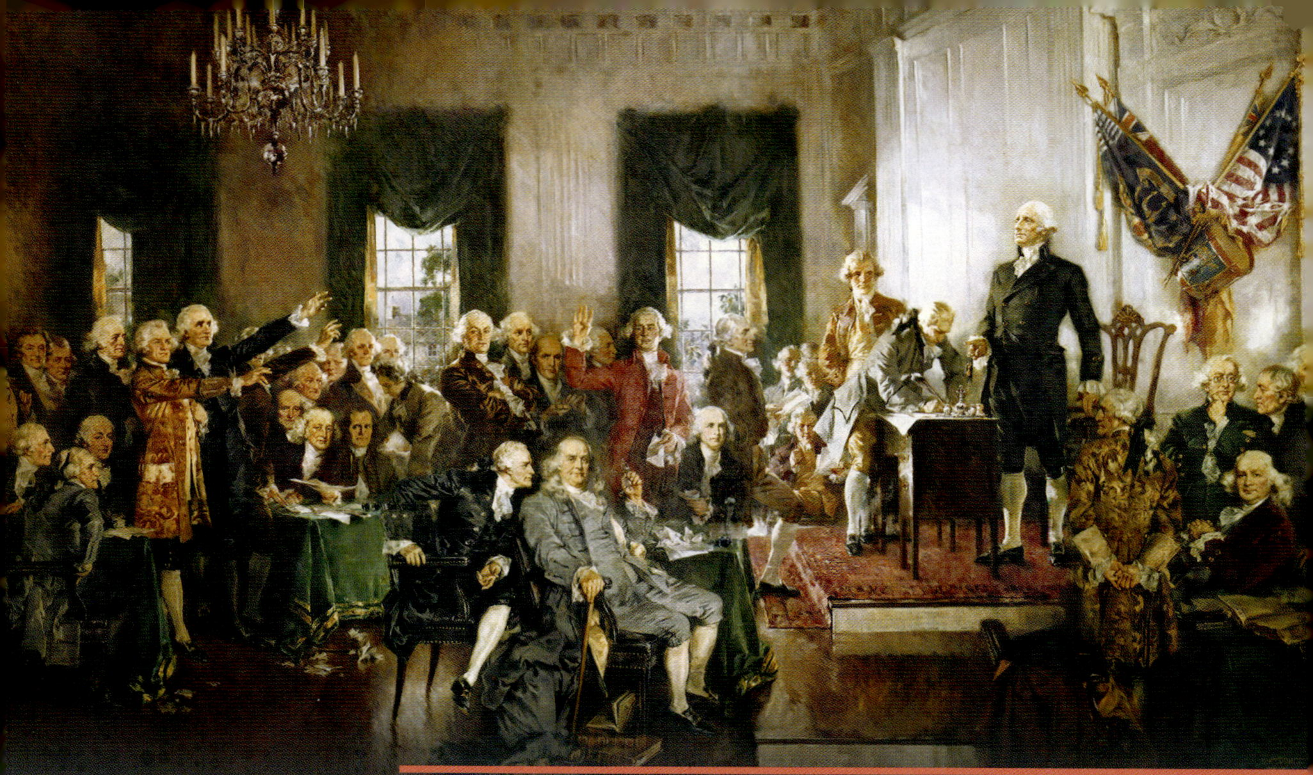

THIS PAINTING OF THE SIGNING OF THE CONSTITUTION IN 1787 HANGS IN THE CAPITOL BUILDING IN WASHINGTON, D.C. ONLY 39 OF THE 55 LEADERS AT THE CONSTITUTIONAL CONVENTION SIGNED THE U.S. CONSTITUTION.

◀ U.S. CONSTITUTION

CONSTITUTIONAL CONVENTION

From May 25 to September 17, 1787, 55 leaders from 12 of the former colonies met for the Constitutional Convention, which was held at the Philadelphia State House in Philadelphia, Pennsylvania. They meant to fix the Articles of Confederation, but ended up framing, or writing, a new constitution.

The framers of the Constitution had escaped the British monarchy and knew what happened when one person or group had too much power. They wanted to protect the American people's independence and make sure the government couldn't take away their rights. They divided the new government into three branches. Each branch has the power to check the other branches to prevent them from having too much power. This keeps them all balanced. That's why it's called a system of checks and balances.

JAMES MADISON WAS THE FOURTH PRESIDENT OF THE UNITED STATES. HE WROTE THE FIRST **DRAFT** OF THE U.S. CONSTITUTION AND WAS VERY CAREFUL TO MAKE SURE THE GOVERNMENT DIDN'T BECOME TOO POWERFUL. HE SAID, "THE TRUTH IS THAT ALL MEN HAVING POWER OUGHT TO BE MISTRUSTED."

JAMES MADISON

THE GREAT COMPROMISE

One problem in setting up the U.S. government was deciding how each state should be represented in Congress. Delegates from the large states felt that the number of representatives should be based on population, but those from small states felt that each state should have the same number of representatives. In the Great **Compromise**, the delegates divided Congress into the Senate, in which each state has two representatives, and the House of Representatives, in which representation is based on each state's population.

Drafting the Articles of Confederation — York Town, Pennsylvania 1777

THE ARTICLES OF CONFEDERATION

The U.S. Constitution is the oldest written national constitution still in use. However, it wasn't the first set of rules in the United States. The Articles of Confederation acted as the first U.S. constitution from 1781 to 1789. Those who wrote the articles made sure they didn't give the federal government too much power. However, the Articles of Confederation weren't effective as a constitution. The federal government had control over the military and foreign affairs, but it had little power to make states follow laws or pay taxes.

Leaders including George Washington, Alexander Hamilton, and James Madison felt the federal government should be stronger. They persuaded the states to send delegates to a Constitutional **Convention** in 1787 to fix the Articles of Confederation.

BOSTON HARBOR

HISTORIC MOMENTS
On December 16, 1773, American patriots dressed as Native Americans snuck onto British East India Company ships delivering tea in Boston Harbor. They threw 342 chests of tea into the harbor to protest taxes on imports and other issues.

MARY LUDWIG HAYS MAY HAVE BEEN MOLLY PITCHER, A LEGENDARY HEROINE OF THE REVOLUTIONARY WAR. SOLDIERS SAID SHE CARRIED PITCHERS OF WATER TO PEOPLE ON THE BATTLEFIELD AND TOOK OVER HER HUSBAND'S PLACE AT A CANNON DURING BATTLE AFTER HE WAS NO LONGER ABLE TO FIGHT.

MOLLY PITCHER

DRAFTING PRESENTATION OF THE DECLARATION OF INDEPENDENCE

A REVOLUTIONARY WAR

The structure of the U.S. government hasn't always been how it is today. When the British first established colonies in eastern North America, these colonies were under British rule. However, the colonists had local leaders and mostly solved their own problems. After a costly war, however, Britain started forcing the colonists to pay new taxes.

The colonists didn't respond well to many of the British **monarchy's** decisions. Eventually, many people decided to fight against Great Britain for the colonies' independence. This was the American Revolutionary War. On July 4, 1776, the Continental Congress, a body of **delegates** from the colonies, approved the Declaration of Independence, creating the United States of America. After many difficult battles, the colonists defeated the British in 1783. The British monarchy no longer had control over them.

CONTENTS

A Revolutionary War 4
The Articles of Confederation 6
Constitutional Convention 8
Separation of Power 10
Legislative Branch 12
Executive Branch 14
Judicial Branch 16
Federalism 18
Keeping the People in Check 20
Presidential Power 22
Avoiding Checks 24
State vs. Federal Law 26
Is Government Balanced? 28
Glossary 31
Index 32
Websites 32

Published in 2019 by The Rosen Publishing Group, Inc.
29 East 21st Street, New York, NY 10010

Copyright © 2019 by The Rosen Publishing Group, Inc.

All rights reserved. No part of this book may be reproduced in any form without permission in writing from the publisher, except by a reviewer.

First Edition

Editor: Elizabeth Krajnik
Book Design: Tanya Dellaccio

Photo Credits: Cover, back cover, pp. 1, 3-32 (background) Tatiana Kasyanova/Shutterstock.com; cover, back cover, pp. 5, 14, 19, 21, 22 (newspaper clipping) STILLFX/Shutterstock.com; cover (Supreme Court building) Diego Grandi/Shutterstock.com; cover (White House) Andrea Izzotti/Shutterstock.com; cover (U.S. Capitol) turtix/Shutterstock.com; p. 5 (top) DEA PICTURE LIBRARY/De Agostini Picture Library/Getty Images; p. 5 (middle) Daniel M. Silva/Shutterstock.com; p. 5 (bottom) https://commons.wikimedia.org/wiki/File:Declaration_of_Independence_(1819),_by_John_Trumbull.jpg; p. 7 (top) Everett - Art/Shutterstock.com; p. 7 (middle) https://commons.wikimedia.org/wiki/File:Articles_page1.jpg; p. 7 (bottom) https://commons.wikimedia.org/wiki/File:Articles_of_Confederation_1977_Issue-13c.jpg; p. 9 (top) https://commons.wikimedia.org/wiki/File:Scene_at_the_Signing_of_the_Constitution_of_the_United_States.jpg; p. 9 (bottom) https://commons.wikimedia.org/wiki/File:Constitution_of_the_United_States,_page_1.jpg; p. 10 Orhan Cam/Shutterstock.com; pp. 11 (top), 29 Joseph Sohm/Shutterstock.com; p. 11 (bottom) chrisukphoto/Shutterstock.com; pp. 13, 17 (bottom) Alex Wong/Getty Images News/Getty Images; p. 15 (top) https://en.wikipedia.org/wiki/File:FDR_1944_Color_Portrait.tif; p. 15 (bottom) https://commons.wikimedia.org/wiki/File:President_Barack_Obama_with_full_cabinet_09-10-09.jpg; p. 17 (top) https://commons.wikimedia.org/wiki/File:Plessy_marker.jpg; p. 19 (top) Justin Sullivan/Getty Images News/Getty Images; p. 19 (bottom) https://en.wikipedia.org/wiki/File:Abraham_Lincoln_O-77_matte_collodion_print.jpg; p. 21 (top) Win McNamee/Getty Images News/Getty Images; p. 21 (bottom) Ethan Miller/Getty Images News/Getty Images; p. 23 (top) https://commons.wikimedia.org/wiki/File:George-W-Bush.jpeg; p. 23 (bottom) PomInOz/Shutterstock.com; p. 25 (top) Corbis/Corbis Historical/Getty Images; p. 25 (bottom) ABDELHAK SENNA/AFP/Getty Images; p. 27 (top) Chuck Wagner/Shutterstock.com; p. 27 (bottom) Blend Images - Hill Street Studios/Brand X Pictures/Getty Images.

Library of Congress Cataloging-in-Publication Data

Names: Honders, Christine, author.
Title: Is the balance of power in government balanced? / Christine Honders.
Description: New York : PowerKids Press, 2019. | Series: Key questions in American history | Includes index.
Identifiers: LCCN 2017054344| ISBN 9781508167587 (library bound) | ISBN 9781508167600 (pbk.) | ISBN 9781508167617 (6 pack)
Subjects: LCSH: Separation of powers–United States–Juvenile literature. | United States–Politics and government–Juvenile literature.
Classification: LCC JK305 .H66 2019 | DDC 320.473/04–dc23
LC record available at https://lccn.loc.gov/2017054344

Manufactured in the United States of America

CPSIA Compliance Information: Batch CS18PK: For Further Information contact Rosen Publishing, New York, New York at 1-800-237-9932

KEY QUESTIONS in AMERICAN HISTORY

IS THE BALANCE OF POWER IN GOVERNMENT BALANCED?

CHRISTINE HONDERS

PowerKiDS press.
New York